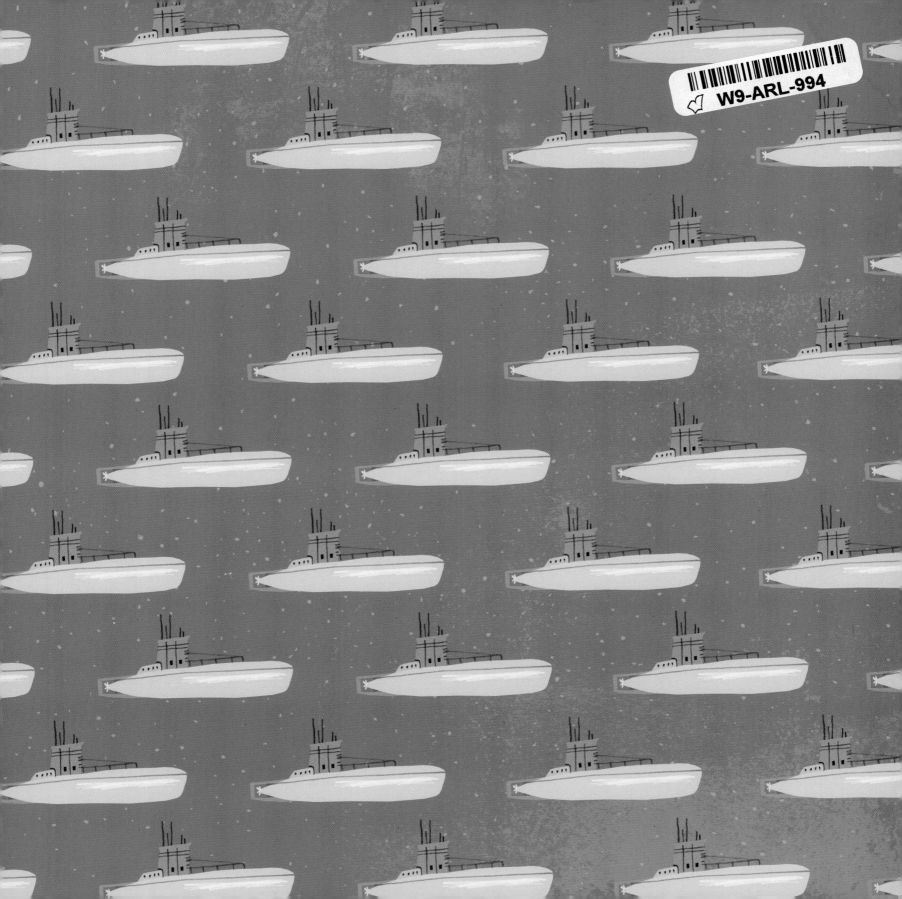

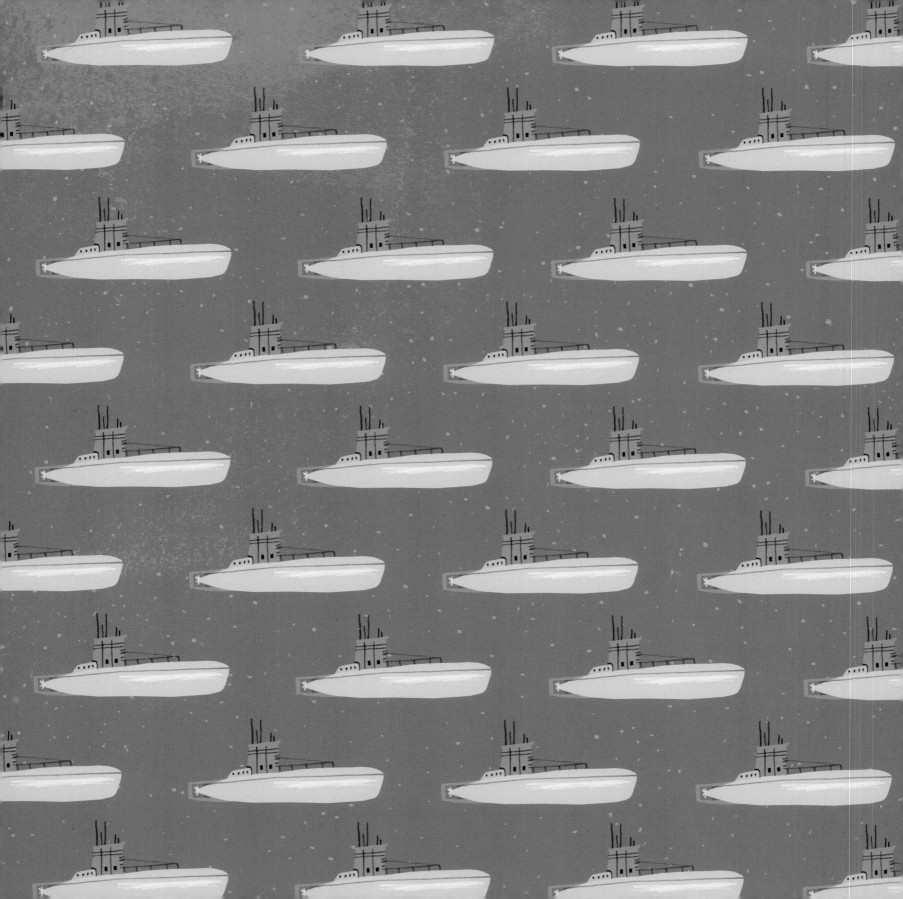

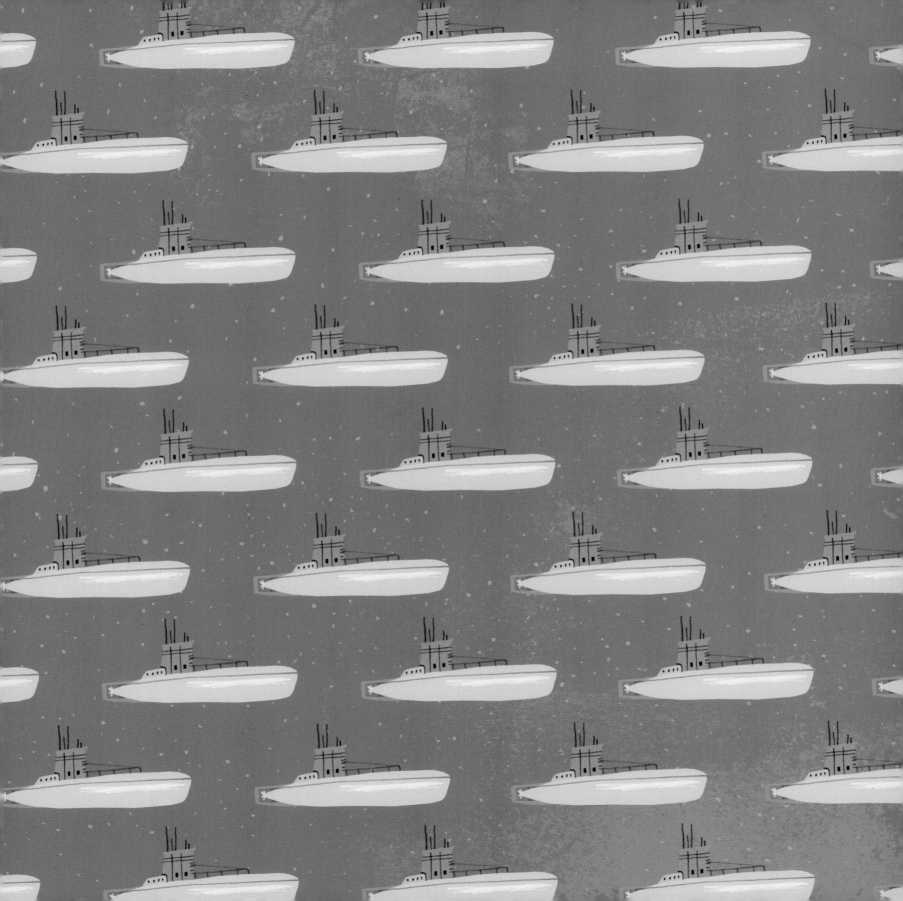

For every child who refuses to strike out.
- J.F.M.

For Rebecca and Rachel
- D.R.

LCCN 2018905032
ISBN 9781943147427 / 9781943147700

Text copyright © 2018 by Julia Finley Mosca
Illustrations by Daniel Rieley
Illustrations copyright © 2018 by The Innovation Press

Published by The Innovation Press
1001 4th Avenue, Suite 3200, Seattle, WA 98154

www.theinnovationpress.com

Printed and bound by Worzalla
Production date: April 2022
Plant location: Stevens Point, Wisconsin

Cover lettering by Nicole LaRue
Cover art by Daniel Rieley
Book layout by Rose Clemens

THE GIRL WITH A MIND FOR MATH

The Story of Raye Montague

WRITTEN BY
JULIA FINLEY MOSCA

ILLUSTRATED BY
DANIEL RIELEY

If there's something you want,
but it seems out of reach,

here's a story for you—
a great truth it will teach.

When you focus your mind,
you'll SUCCEED through and through,

like one bold ENGINEER
by the name MONTAGUE.

In a state we call ARKANSAS,
one winter day,

a baby was welcomed—
a GIRL they called RAYE.

She was bright as a star,
super SMART from the start.

She was HEADSTRONG, this child,
and not faint of heart.

Yes, this girl had POTENTIAL.
Her granddad was proud.

He told her, "Work hard. You'll
stand out from the crowd."

Then something she'd cherish—
when Raye was just seven,

he took her to see her first SHIP.
It was heaven.

"A real SUBMARINE!"
Her eyes opened wide.

"Who made it?" she asked,
as they followed the guide.

"ENGINEERS," said the man,
giving Raye's head a pat.

"But my dear, YOU don't need
to know all about that."

At the time, the man's insult
went over her head.

"No, you CAN'T," were the words
he had meant, but not said.

"Engineering," thought Raye, and her life's DREAM began.

Except most people laughed when she told them her plan.

"Stay STRONG," said her mom.
"Use your BRAINS. You'll be fine.

There will always be people
who pay you no mind—

just because you're a girl,
and because you are black.

Don't let them or the state of
your SCHOOL hold you back."

You see, schools in those days
were what's called SEGREGATED.

The black and white students
were kept SEPARATED.

"That's WRONG!" you exclaim.
It was dismal, no fooling.

And worst of all, white kids
received better schooling.

But Raye studied hard.
She had GRIT—taught herself.

She was gifted in MATH
and read books by the shelf.

When the time came for COLLEGE,
she knew what to choose.

She'd learn to build BOATS!
But she got some bad news . . .

"Engineering's not taught
to black students," they said.

Her heart hit the floor.
"I'll take BUSINESS instead."

She'd learn what she could,
and she'd learn the rest later.

Their rules were unjust,
but that school wouldn't break her.

Raye finished with HONORS!
Oh boy, what a smarty.

She said her farewells
(there was no time to party).

"I'm off to a place filled
with HISTORY's greats—

the CAPITAL CITY
of all fifty states!"

Now, finding a JOB?
It turned out that took time.

She looked and she looked.
Raye was not one to whine.

Then it must have been fate
(at least, that's what it seems);

she was hired to TYPE
where they built . . . SUBMARINES!

The NAVY! That's right!
Oh, but hold all your cheers.

Ship designing was only
for TRAINED engineers.

So, she watched as they worked,
and she learned every task,

even studied COMPUTERS
by night in a class.

Then her BIG BREAK arrived—
the whole staff got the flu.

Raye did all of her work . . .
and the engineers' too!

Her boss was in shock.
"H-H-HOW?!" he exploded.

"From MEMORY," said Raye.
And with that, got promoted.

Life should've been swell,
yet that wasn't the case.

Her boss treated her poorly
because of her race.

MANY people, like him,
tried to make her feel small.

Raye just held her head high,
and she OUTWORKED them all.

What next? From the White House there came a command.

The PRESIDENT ordered a SHIP: "Make it GRAND—

and QUICKLY," he added. Well, that didn't fly.

All those plans would take engineers MONTHS to supply.

Here's the thing about that:
when designing a boat,

there are thousands of
MEASUREMENTS one needs to note.

All those numbers take MATH,
and that takes some time.

Ah, but Raye had been working
on something sublime.

```
ACT 1: PROC (NUM 1) RECURSIVE;
DCL NUM 1 FIXED BIN (15,0);
IF NUM 1 < = 1  THEN
  RETURN (1);
 ELSE
  RETURN (NUM 1* FACT * (N    1 -1));
ND FACT 1;
```

She took a deep breath . . .
"I can solve this," she said.

"I've come up with a SYSTEM
to do it instead.

It'll draw the plans FASTER,"
she told them. "Don't fret.

I'LL DESIGN THE FIRST SHIP
BY COMPUTER! No sweat."

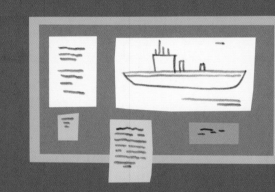

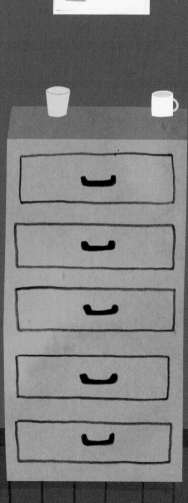

How long do you think that might take?
What's your guess?

Would it take her a month?
Maybe weeks for success?

Well, it took CALCULATIONS
(and tons of caffeine),

but Raye finished in HOURS . . .
just over EIGHTEEN!

Her program—it WORKED!
All the blueprints were done.

The ship was constructed.
The engineers? STUNNED.

"YOU DID IT!" they cheered,
and her boss had to say

that her quick mind for math
had in fact saved the day.

The end? No, not quite.
When Raye's ship was unveiled,

only white men could go.
And Raye's invite? NOT mailed.

Say WHAAATT?!!
You heard right.

No invite?!
ABHORRIBLE!

In fact, some might say
it was downright DEPLORABLE.

Yet Raye kept her cool—
gave her best every day,

and in time all her SKILLS
were applauded. HOORAY!

People learned of her work.
"Who's this Raye?" they'd demand.

When they met her, they stared.
They expected a MAN!

Yes, that happened a lot.
Many could not believe

that a WOMAN of COLOR
did all she'd achieved.

Some even thought Raye
was a maid (sad, but true).

When they ordered a drink,
she'd say, "Bring me one too!"

All her HUMOR and WIT
served her well through the years,

as she battled the hard times
with LAUGHS and not tears.

And that boss in the NAVY
who'd been so unkind . . .

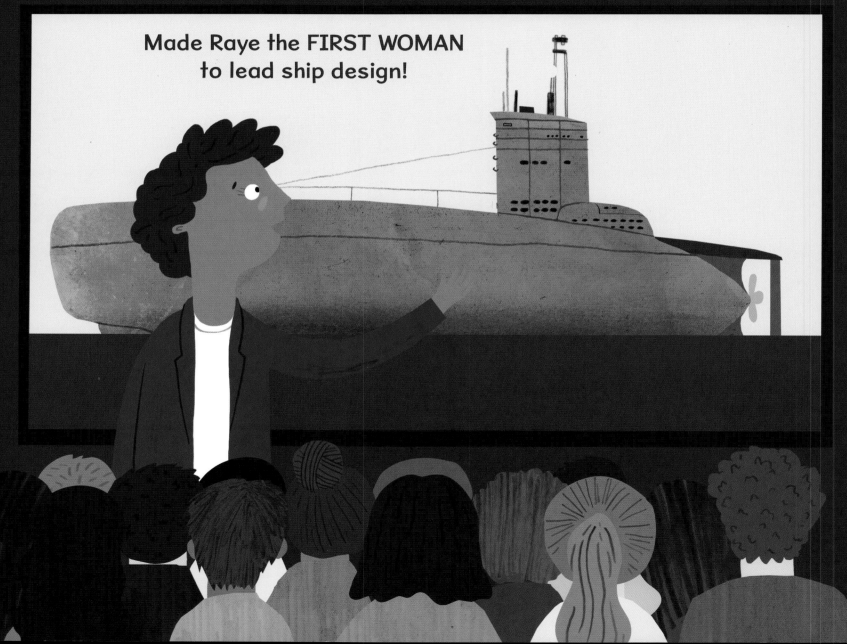

Made Raye the FIRST WOMAN
to lead ship design!

More honors would follow.
Her fame picked up steam.

And finally, at last,
she accomplished her DREAM.

That title she'd worked for—
an ENGINEER! SCORRRRE!!

Now the world knows her FEATS.
She is hidden no more.

RAYE MONTAGUE
Engineer

So, the lesson to ALL
is don't ever give in.

Take a CHANCE. Rock the boat.
If it sinks, you can SWIM.

When a storm comes your way,
hold your course, and don't stress.

NEVER QUIT, and like Raye,
PROPEL STRAIGHT TO SUCCESS!

Dear Reader,

If you have a dream like I did, study hard and stay focused!

Always remember that just because someone says "you can't," that doesn't have to stop you. You might have to go in a different direction, and it might take you a little longer, but you CAN achieve your dreams!

Raye Montague

FACTS AND TIDBITS FROM THE AUTHOR'S CHAT WITH RAYE!

Circumnavigating the Norms

"I didn't really like dolls," Montague said when asked about her favorite hobbies as a child. "Luckily, my mother and grandfather always encouraged my love of math, science, and thinking outside the box. They taught me there was no such thing as women's work or men's work." In high school, Montague's mother even convinced the principal to let her daughter test out of home economics.

"My mother was the wind beneath my wings," she said. Using her photographic memory, Montague studied the coursework and was able to pass all of the exams without taking the class. She took extra math and science classes instead!

Raye's mother, Flossie

Paddling Haters with Humor

If there's one principle Montague followed throughout her career, it's that you can't let others bring you down. "People say very negative things. If you let it fester, then they control you," she explained. "You must always have a comeback ready—a humorous comeback—that allows you to take back control of the situation." She recalled one meeting where a man attempted to order a cup of coffee—confusing her for someone who had been hired to wait on him (which happened frequently). Rather than get angry, she said, "I'll take one too. Make mine with cream and sugar."

Another time, while traveling with her white colleagues during a time when many places were still segregated, she was informed she would need to find a room at a different hotel. "That's okay. I don't need a room. Just give me a pull-out and I'll sleep right here," she told the staff. Since they didn't want Montague sleeping in their lobby, they gave her the only room they had left . . . the penthouse!

Propelling Through Misperceptions

A maid and a secretary weren't the only people Montague was mistaken for over the years. "Everybody just assumed I was a white man because of my name," she said. "I was hired many times sight unseen, and when people met me, they couldn't believe it." When she finally received her engineer's license later on in her career, it read "based on *his* qualifications." Despite the confusion, Montague believes her parents' decision to give her a gender-neutral name was a positive, and it's a family tradition that continues. "The reason my granddaughter (Riley) has an androgynous name is because my son (Dr. David Montague) saw so many doors opened for me." Montague added that her granddaughter also hopes to pursue a career in the STEM fields. "She wants to find a cure for cancer!"

Sailing Despite the Storms

Though she overcame sexism and racism from many colleagues, Montague's road to success was far from easy. One of her earliest bosses in the navy was especially hard on the young business graduate. "He was really racist," Montague recalled. "When he came in and saw that I was female and black, I imagine he thought, 'Oh my God, how am I going to get rid of her?'" Convinced she would fail, he gave her six months to complete a project that the navy had been working on for six years—modifying a computer system to design ships. "Little did I know, people had said it was an impossible goal," Montague explained. Never one to balk at a challenge, she taught herself to drive and went to the office every night, working overtime on the project for free. When her boss forbid her from being there alone, she brought her mother and son with her, telling him, "You said I couldn't work alone, so I'm not alone!" Finally, when she believed she had perfected the system, that boss had a harsh surprise. "He said, 'Nobody's gonna use it, Raye.' I was devastated. That really hurt."

Only two weeks later, things would change when President Nixon gave the navy just two months to design a new ship. Montague's boss came straight to her with the task. Using her newly perfected computer program, she completed the draft in just over eighteen hours. "The boss fell in love with me, because so much of the honor went to him," she said. "After that, he opened many doors for me, and really set me up to take over his position." Many years later, Montague would receive another sign of affection from her once-combative superior. "When he died, his wife called me and said, 'Raye, he asked for YOU to plan his funeral' . . . I think that I changed his mind totally about racism."

Anchoring a Spot in History

Perhaps the most shocking example of racism in Montague's career happened not long after she completed that groundbreaking ship design. "I wasn't even invited to the launch," she said. It was a despicable snub, but Montague remained confident that history would give her the credit she deserved. "I felt that eventually it would come." And come it did. Yet, when asked about racism in our current society, Montague was a realist. "We've made some progress, but we still have a long way to go . . . I believe education will do it, but I still run into people who think that because I'm black, I couldn't really have done all these things." So what did the spitfire scientist tell all those skeptics? "Google me!"

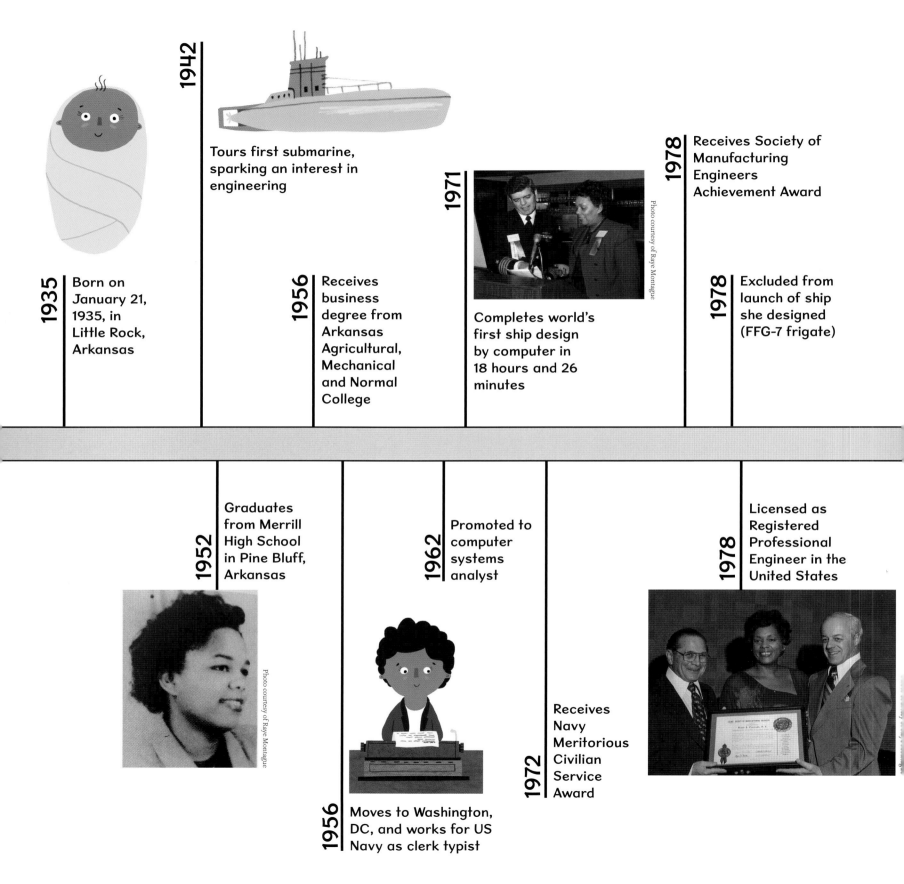

1942
Tours first submarine, sparking an interest in engineering

1935
Born on January 21, 1935, in Little Rock, Arkansas

1956
Receives business degree from Arkansas Agricultural, Mechanical and Normal College

1971
Completes world's first ship design by computer in 18 hours and 26 minutes

Photo courtesy of Raye Montague

1978
Receives Society of Manufacturing Engineers Achievement Award

1978
Excluded from launch of ship she designed (FFG-7 frigate)

1952
Graduates from Merrill High School in Pine Bluff, Arkansas

Photo courtesy of Raye Montague

1962
Promoted to computer systems analyst

1956
Moves to Washington, DC, and works for US Navy as clerk typist

1972
Receives Navy Meritorious Civilian Service Award

1978
Licensed as Registered Professional Engineer in the United States

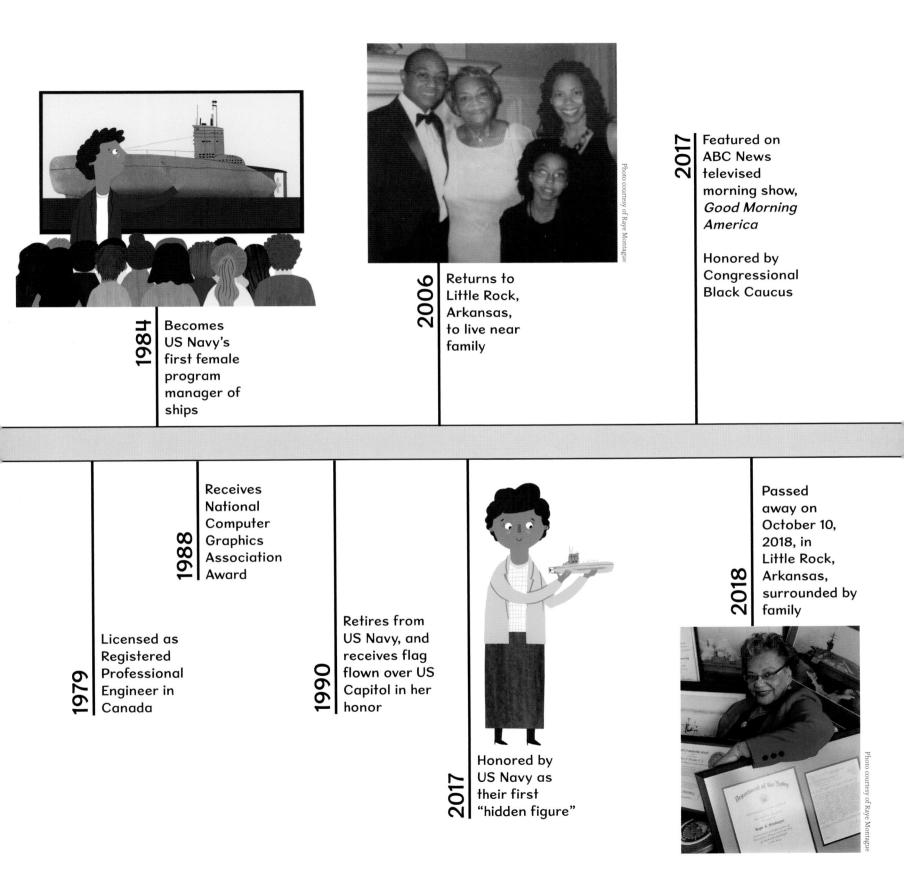

1984
Becomes US Navy's first female program manager of ships

2006
Returns to Little Rock, Arkansas, to live near family

Photo courtesy of Raye Montague

2017
Featured on ABC News televised morning show, *Good Morning America*

Honored by Congressional Black Caucus

1979
Licensed as Registered Professional Engineer in Canada

1988
Receives National Computer Graphics Association Award

1990
Retires from US Navy, and receives flag flown over US Capitol in her honor

2017
Honored by US Navy as their first "hidden figure"

2018
Passed away on October 10, 2018, in Little Rock, Arkansas, surrounded by family

Photo courtesy of Raye Montague

ABOUT RAYE MONTAGUE

Raye Jean Jordan Montague was born on January 21, 1935, in Little Rock, Arkansas, to parents Rayford Jordan and Flossie Graves Jordan. The internationally registered professional engineer had a long and successful career as a civilian employee with the US Navy, although she battled racism and sexism every step of the way. Many of Montague's accomplishments went unrecognized by the general public for decades, until she was finally credited worldwide as the first person to design a ship using a computer. She also made history as the Navy's first female program manager of ships.

Prior to the start of the Civil Rights Movement, black children (especially girls) had very few role models in professional occupations. Luckily, Montague had a supportive network of family members and mentors. Noticing her interest in math and science, her grandfather, Thomas Graves, encouraged her to pursue those subjects. When she was just seven years old, he took her to downtown Little Rock to see a World War II German submarine that had been captured off the coast of the Carolinas. Entranced by the boat, she asked a white tour guide what she needed to learn in order to design one like it. The man informed her that one would have to study engineering, but that she didn't need to worry about that—implying that a girl of color could never do such a thing. Ignoring his dismissal, Montague set her sights on becoming an engineer.

Photo courtesy of Raye Montague

Along with her grandfather, Montague's mother was instrumental in her pursuit of this new goal. Mrs. Jordan told her daughter that although she was up against three strikes from society—her gender, her race, and her segregated schooling—she could achieve any dream with a good education. That advice, while wise, wasn't so easy to follow. One of the many drawbacks of segregation was that schools for black students frequently received secondhand resources from white schools, such as torn and tattered textbooks with missing pages. In addition, black educators were often prevented from pursuing advanced degrees like those of their white counterparts. Thankfully, many of Montague's instructors were extremely motivated and bright. With their guidance, as well as her own dedication to learning, she excelled.

In 1952, after graduating from Merrill High School in Pine Bluff, Montague was heartbroken to discover that none of the colleges in her surrounding area admitted black students into their engineering programs. Since her mother couldn't afford to send her away to school, she decided to study business at Arkansas Agricultural, Mechanical and Normal College (now the University of Arkansas at Pine Bluff). She obtained her degree with honors in 1956 and hopped on a train to Washington, DC, in search of work.

Montague's journey to the East Coast was the first time she had ever traveled out of her home state of Arkansas. While she hadn't yet secured a job, she had faith that the capital city would be the best place for opportunity. As luck would have it, her first offer came from the US Navy—the branch of the military that operates fleets of submarines! Montague was initially hired as a clerk typist, but she quickly took advantage of the chance to work within close proximity to engineers. Using the photographic memory she had discovered at a young age, she studied and memorized many of their tasks, including how to use a UNIVAC I, the world's first commercial computer. At night, she expanded her knowledge by taking courses in computer programming.

One fateful day, all of the engineers in Montague's department called in sick, and with the skills she'd learned, she was able to do their work. Her boss was shocked, but impressed, and promoted her to the position of computer systems analyst. Although it was a boost in status, Montague continued to be plagued by sexism and racism. She was held to unrealistic standards and was frequently asked to overcome obstacles set up to intimidate her. As a woman and person of color, she was also sometimes mistaken for a secretary or maid. Montague has credited her positive attitude and sense of humor for helping her push forward during these hurtful times. She worked doubly hard to meet every challenge thrown her way—even putting in extra hours and night shifts for free.

Montague's greatest career achievement occurred in 1971, when President Nixon ordered the navy to build a ship in only two months. At that time, blueprints for a boat normally took engineers up to two years to draw by hand. Fortunately, she had been working on modifying some existing automated computer systems to do the job instead. Much to the surprise of her colleagues, she was successful. Using her newly perfected system, Montague completed the design for the FFG-7 frigate (the Oliver Hazard Perry class) in a record eighteen hours and twenty-six minutes, making her the first person in the world to design a ship by computer. Sadly, due to racist and sexist attitudes at the time, her work was passed up to the president through her white male superiors, and many outside of her department weren't aware of her role in the project. Racism also kept the brilliant mathematician from being invited when the ship finally launched in 1978.

Despite these oversights, Montague's work did not go completely ignored. She was promoted and rewarded several times for her incredible advancements in ship design. She received the Navy Meritorious Civilian Service Award in 1972 and the Society of Manufacturing Engineers Achievement Award in 1978. After years of doing the job of an engineer, she was made a registered professional engineer in both the United States (1978) and Canada (1979)—something very few in her profession had achieved. In 1984, Montague accepted the role of the US Navy's very first female program manager of ships, managing teams of up to two hundred and fifty people, and in 1988, she received the National Computer Graphics Association Award for the Advancement of Computer Graphics. When she retired in 1990, Montague was bestowed with what she calls one of her greatest accolades to date—a flag that flew over the nation's Capitol building in her honor. Yet even with all of these accomplishments, it would be many more years before her groundbreaking contributions went public on a larger scale.

In 2006, the scientific pioneer returned to Arkansas to be near her son and family. It was there that she finally began getting the global recognition she deserved—receiving numerous honors and awards from esteemed groups and institutions like the Congressional Black Caucus and the University of Oklahoma, which established an engineering scholarship in her name. In 2017, she was a featured guest on the nationally televised morning show, Good Morning America, and that same year she returned to Washington, DC, to address the Navy. While there, the military branch officially dubbed her the first of their very own "hidden figures," a reference to the 2016 award-winning Hollywood movie by the same name. At the age of 83, Montague passed away on October 10, 2018, in Little Rock, surrounded by her loved ones.

Throughout her life, Montague was often quoted giving the wise advice a teacher once gave her: "Aim for the stars. At the very least, you'll land on the moon." Though that teacher would undoubtedly agree that her former student's feats were cosmic, Montague always claimed that she never realized she was breaking glass ceilings—she was just doing what she needed to do in order to reach her goals. It was this genuine humility, dedication, and unwavering perseverance that truly made Raye Montague one of history's most inspiring AMAZING SCIENTISTS.

Acknowledgements

The publisher, author, and illustrator are immensely grateful to Raye Montague for speaking at length with the author, contributing personal photos, and providing helpful commentary throughout the creation of this book.

Bibliography

Articles

Faller, Angelita. "Montague Mother and Son Duo Say Education is the Key to Breaking Barriers." *University News*, University of Arkansas at Little Rock, February 24, 2017. http://ualr.edu/news/2017/02/24/david-raye-montague-breaking-barriers.

Miller, Sharde. "Meet the Woman Who Broke Barriers as a Hidden Figure at the US Navy." ABC News, February 20, 2017. https://abcnews.go.com/Entertainment/meet-woman-broke-barriers-hidden-figure-us-navy/story?id=45566924.

Naval Sea Systems Command. "When the Chips Fall, Be Ready & Take Charge – Navy's 'Hidden Figure' Advises Audience." April 19, 2017. http://www.navsea.navy.mil/Media/News/Article/1156653/when-the-chips-fall-be-ready-take-charge-navys-hidden-figure-advisesaudience.

Books

Shetterly, Margot Lee. *Hidden Figures Illustrated Edition: The American Dream and the Untold Story of the Black Women Mathematicians Who Helped Win the Space Race.* New York: William Morrow and Company, 2017. Print.

Shetterly, Margot Lee. *Hidden Figures Young Readers' Edition.* New York: HarperCollins, 2016. Print.

Videos/Film

Good Morning America. "Hidden Figures – Janelle Monae Interview." *YouTube* video, 2:42. February 20, 2017. https://www.youtube.com/watch?v=KBEBDpnpk5Q.

Naval Sea Systems Command. "A Conversation with Raye Montague – Part 1." *YouTube* video, 27:52. April 14, 2017. https://www.youtube.com/watch?v=cNR1IOQX0Ok.

Naval Sea Systems Command. "A Conversation with Raye Montague – Part 2." *YouTube* video, 30:05. April 14, 2017. https://www.youtube.com/watch?v=6MVjtNCYFjo.

Weiss, Suzannah. "This Woman Was the Navy's 'Hidden Figure.'" Refinery 29 video, 9:59. February 20, 2017. https://www.refinery29.com/2017/02/141803/hidden-figures-navy-raye-montague.

Websites

Hidden Figures
http://www.hiddenfigures.com

United States Navy
https://www.navy.com

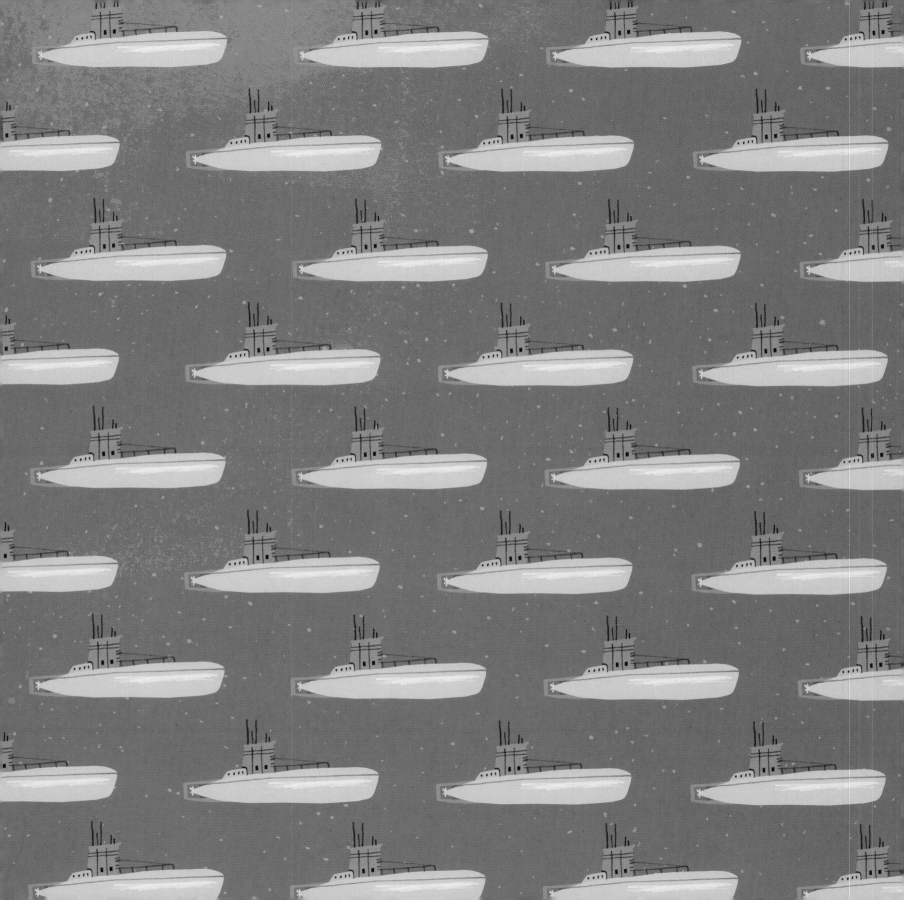

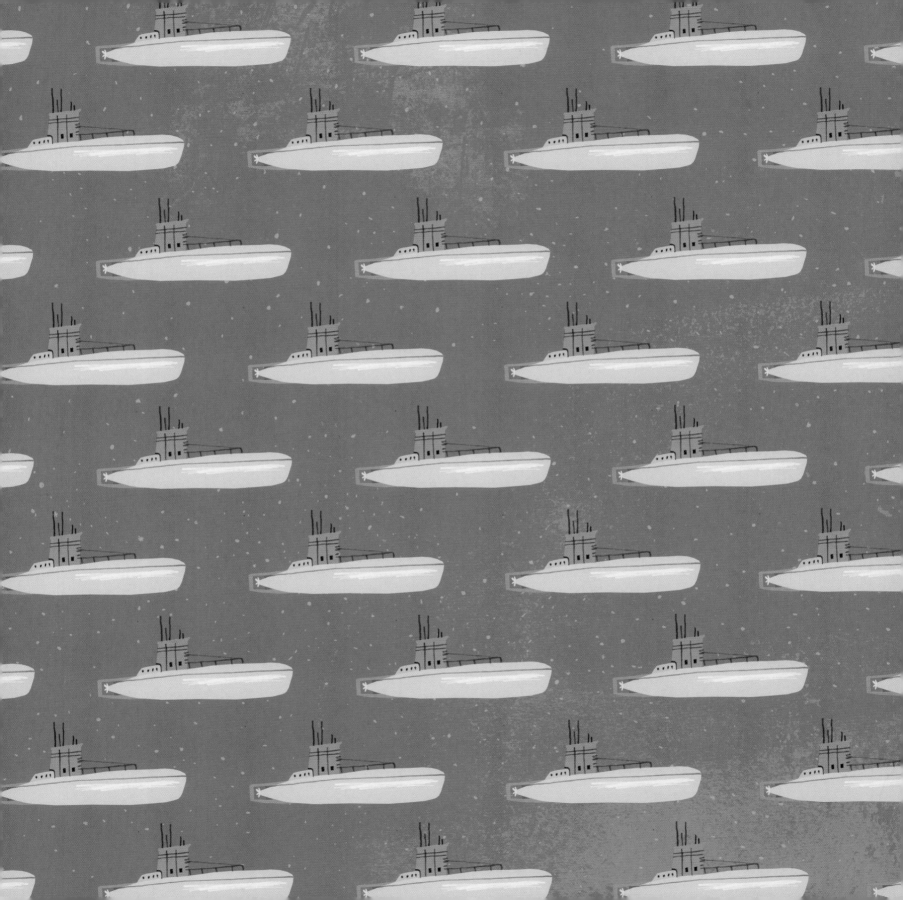

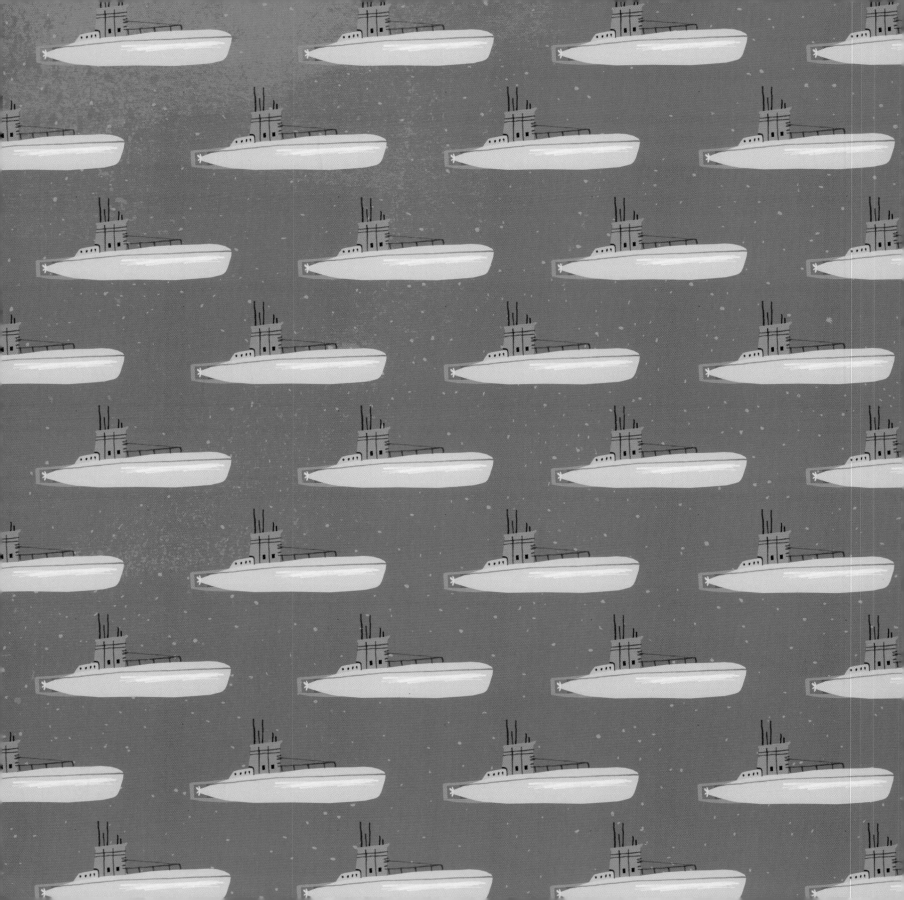